THE GOOD SAMARITAN

Retold by Jean Horton Berg

Illustrated by Gordon Laite

Coloration by Ellen Crouch

Recorded songs by Merle Witham Miller

© 1975 The Christian Science Publishing Society

All rights reserved

ISBN 0-87510-101-1

Printed in the United States of America

The Bible has given us two very important laws.
It tells us "Thou shalt love the Lord thy God
　with all thy heart, and with all thy soul,
　　and with all thy strength, and with all thy mind;

　and thy neighbour as thyself."

One time a man asked Jesus, "Who is my neighbor?"
Jesus answered the man by telling a parable—
　a story—called "The Good Samaritan."
You can read it in the book of Luke in the Bible.

Here is how "The Good Samaritan" might be told today.

Once upon a time a certain man was traveling on the steep and lonely, rocky road from Jerusalem to Jericho.

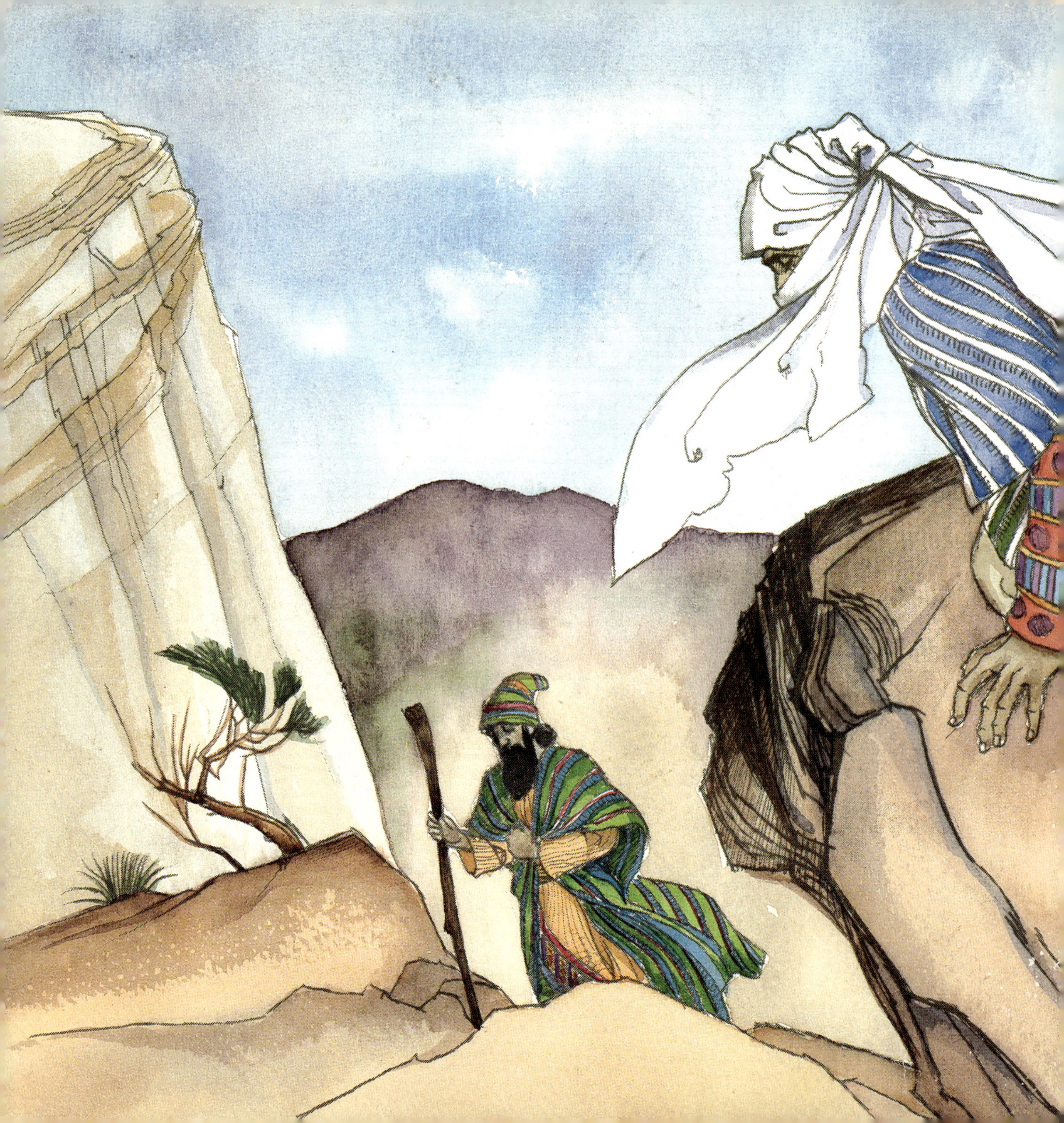

He was trudging along minding his own business, when suddenly a band of wicked thieves rushed out and pounced on him.

They knocked him down and beat him.
They tore his good clothes,
  grabbed his money and ran away.

The man was so badly hurt
  that he couldn't even get up from the ground.

The poor fellow just lay helpless
  in the middle of the road for a long time.

After a while a priest from the temple in Jerusalem
came tramping along that steep
and lonely, rocky road.

He glanced at the man lying there.
And without so much as slowing down,
he tramped right past.

"You certainly see some sad things
on the road," he murmured.
And he hurried on his way.

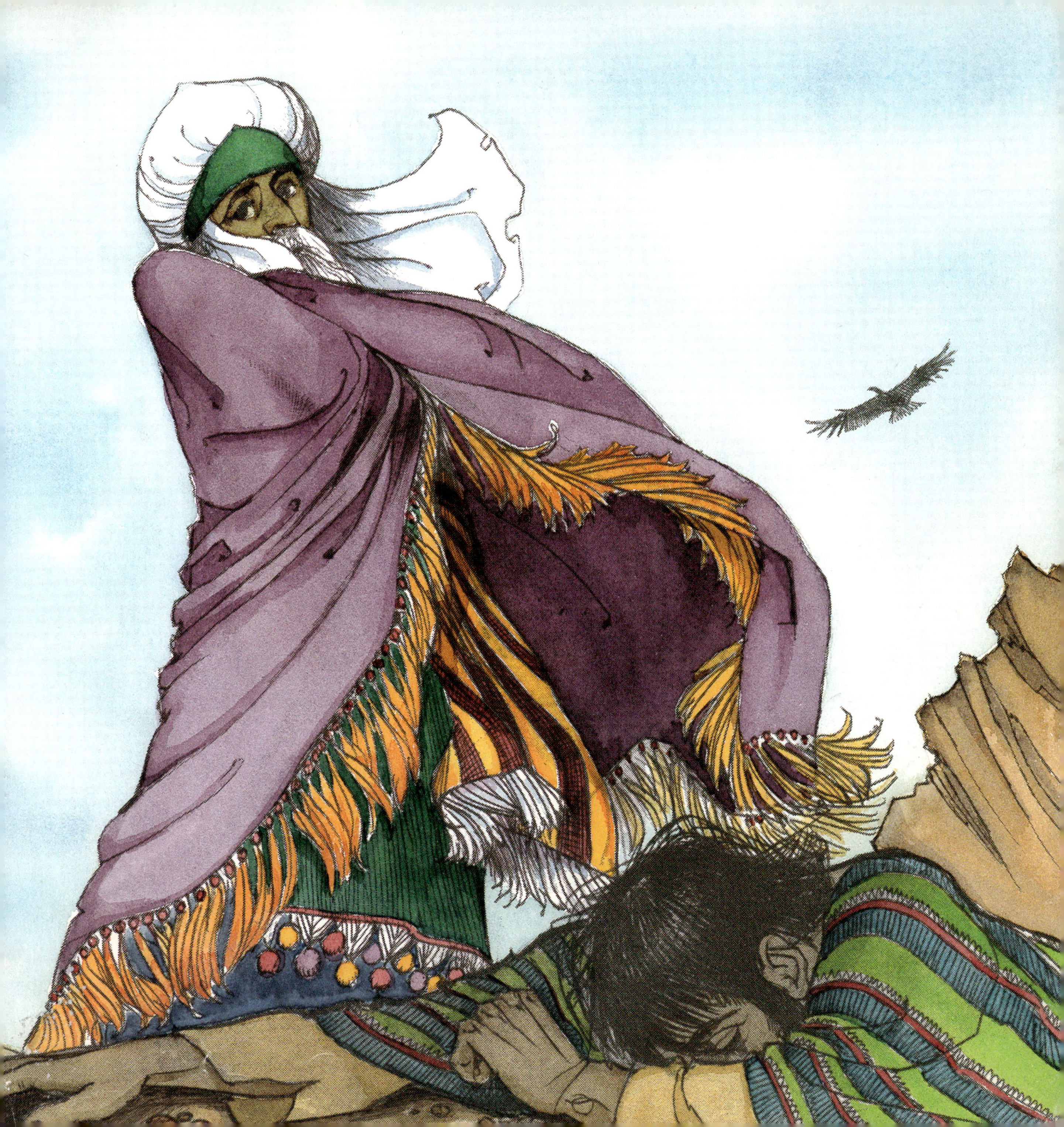

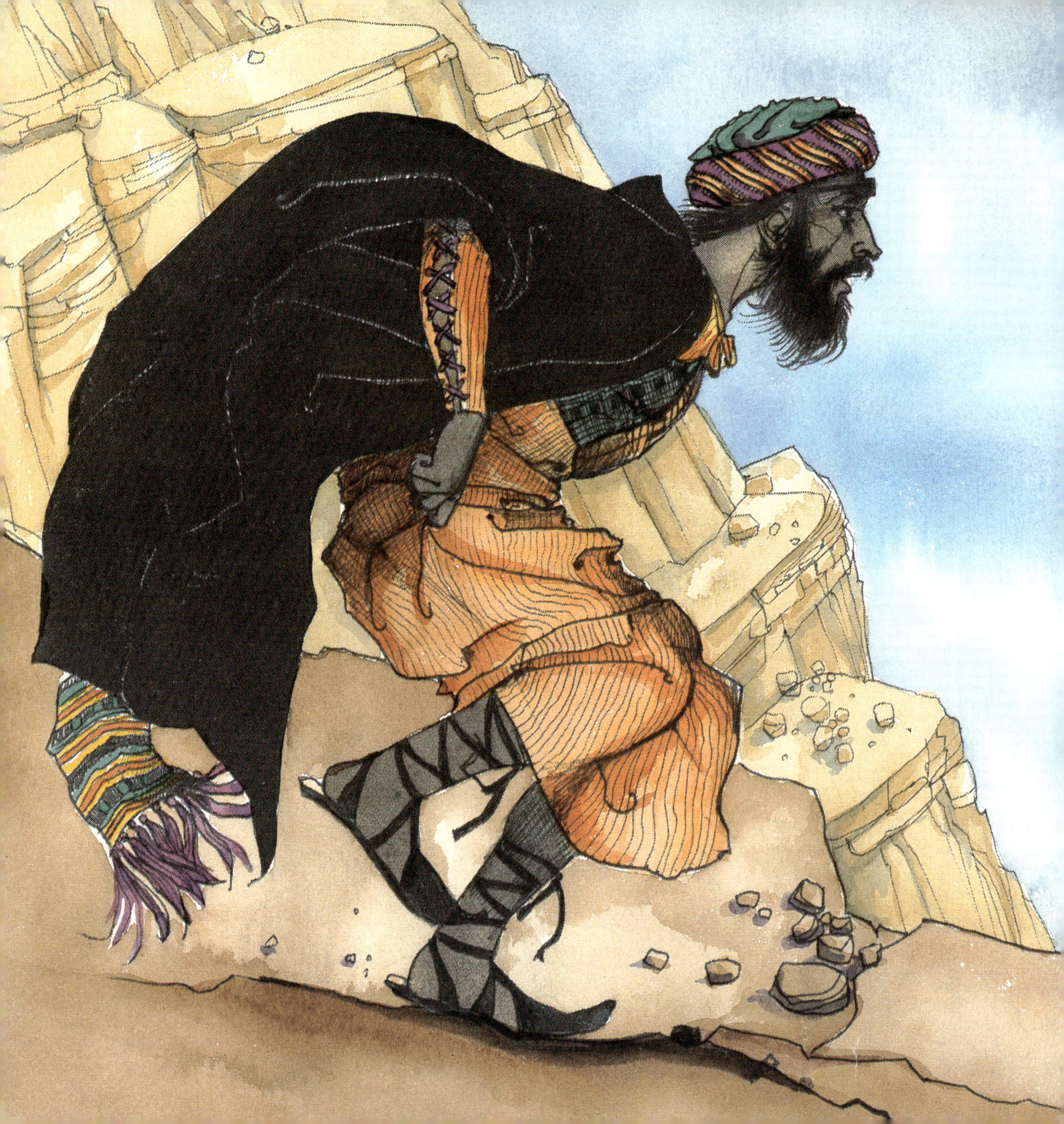

Pretty soon a Levite, a helper in the temple,
  came marching along that steep
  and lonely, rocky road.
"Hmm," he said, looking ahead,
  "What's that big lump
  of something in the middle of the road?
Could it be a rock or an animal?"

He ran up eagerly to see what it was.

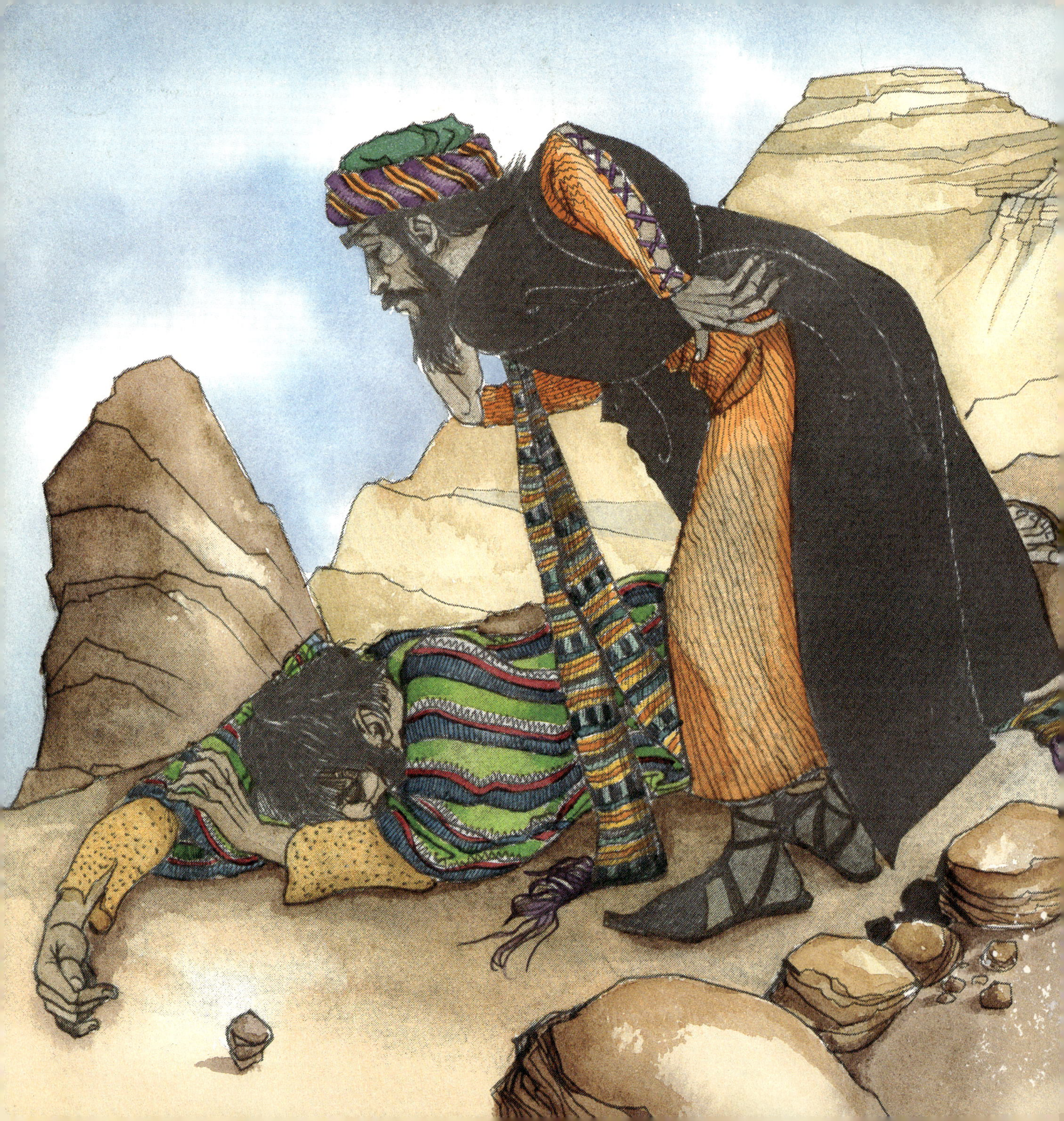

When he saw that the lump of something
   was a man lying hurt,
   he clucked sadly.
"Tsk, tsk, tsk, tsk. What a pity."
Then he looked more closely and said,
   "Isn't he a sorry sight!

He doesn't look like anyone I know.
I wonder if he goes to the temple at Jerusalem."

Then, with never a backward glance,
he hurried on his way.

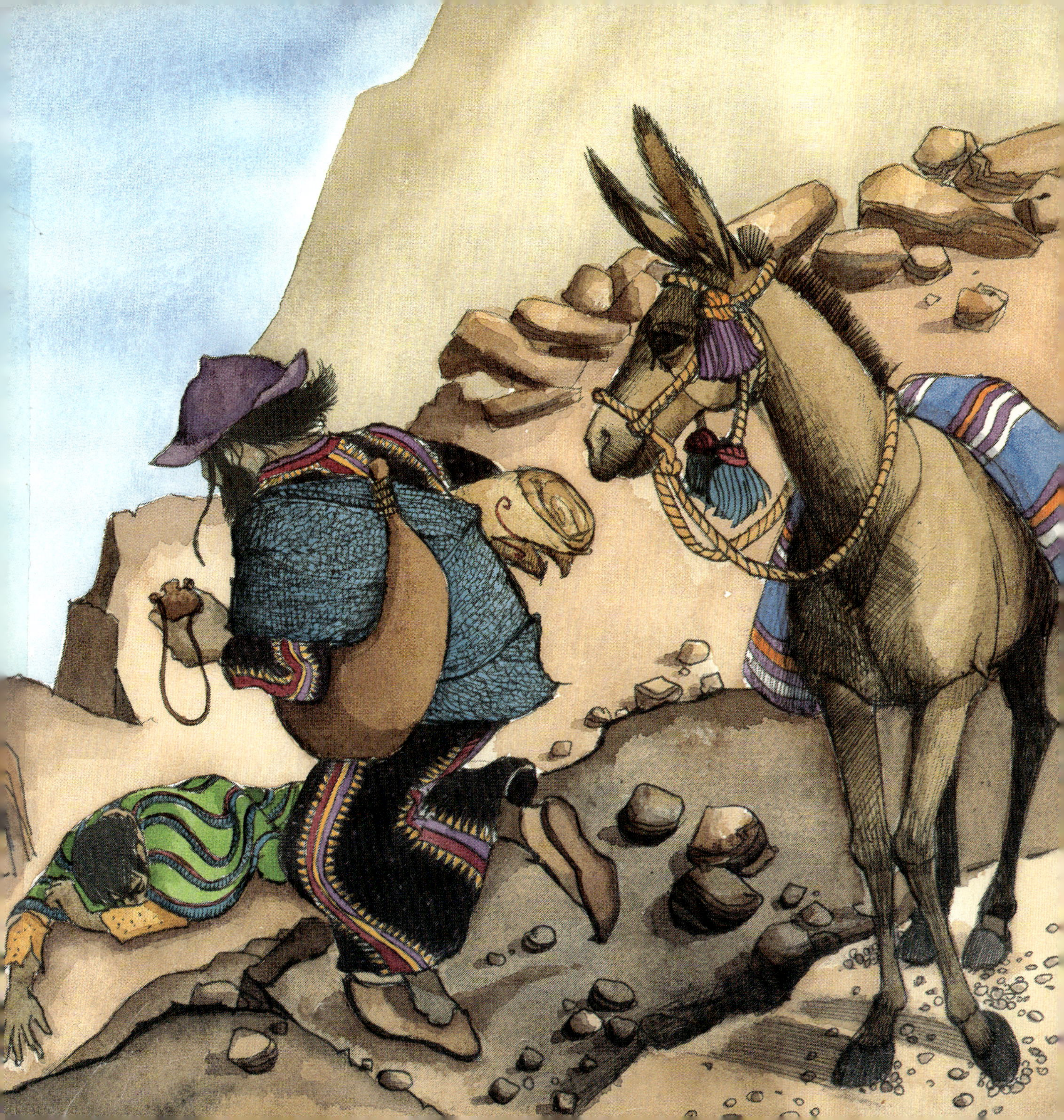

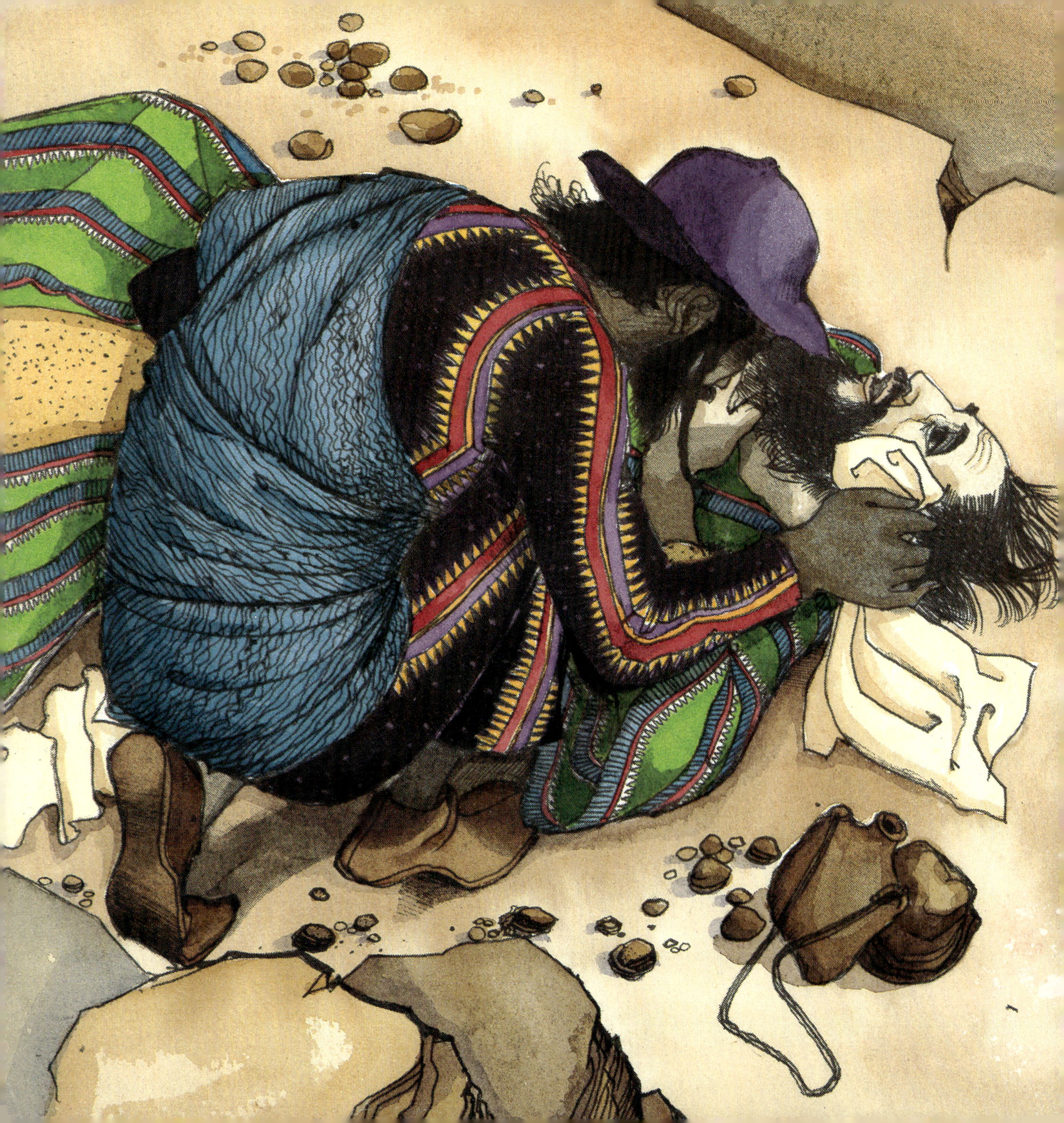

He cleaned the man's wounds
and covered them carefully.

Then he lifted him gently
onto the donkey's back,
and took the man to an inn
where he took care of him.

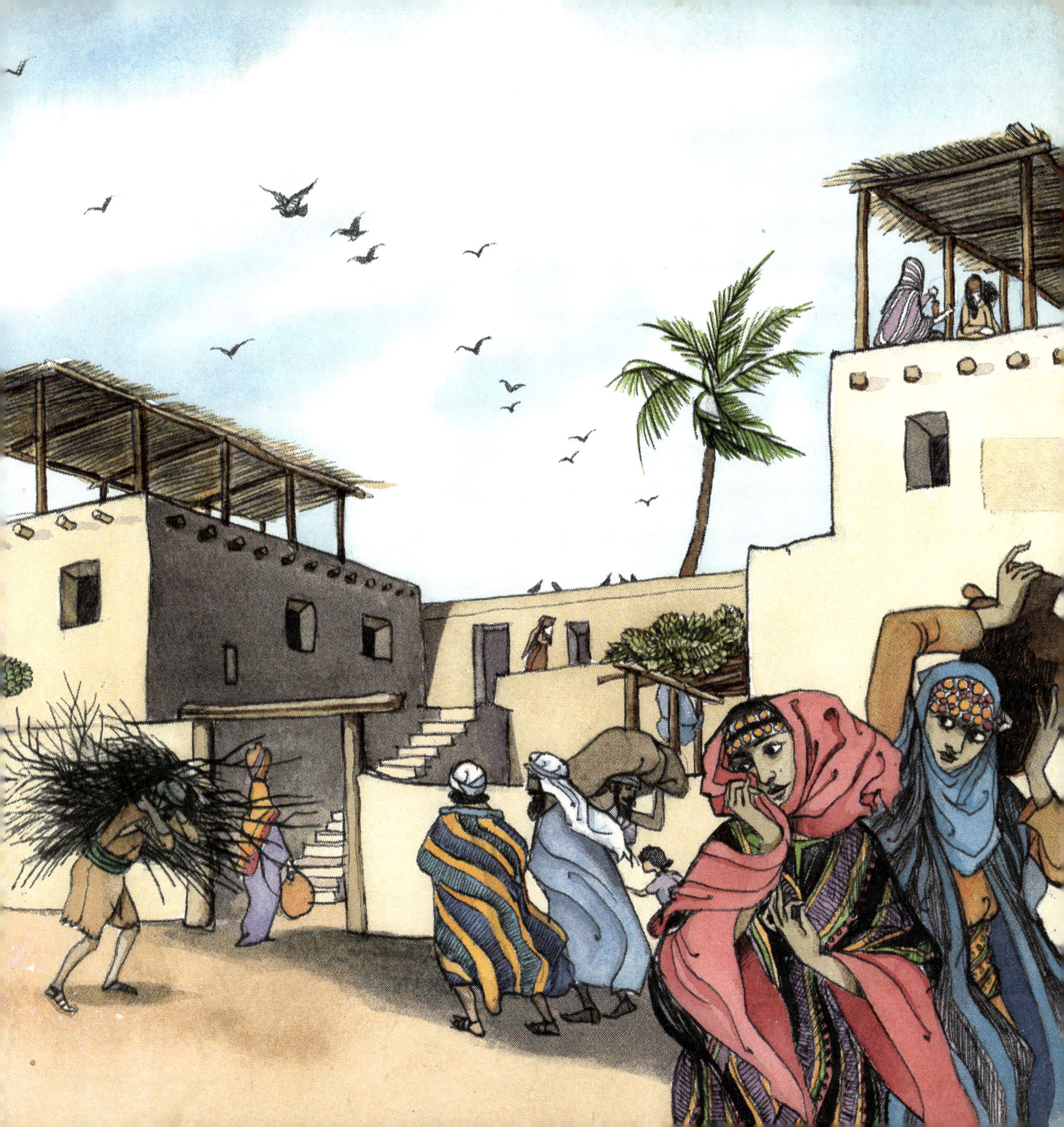

The next day the Samaritan
   gave the innkeeper some money.
"I can't stay here any longer," he said.
"I really have to go on to Jericho today.
Take this money.
Use what you need to take good care of our friend.

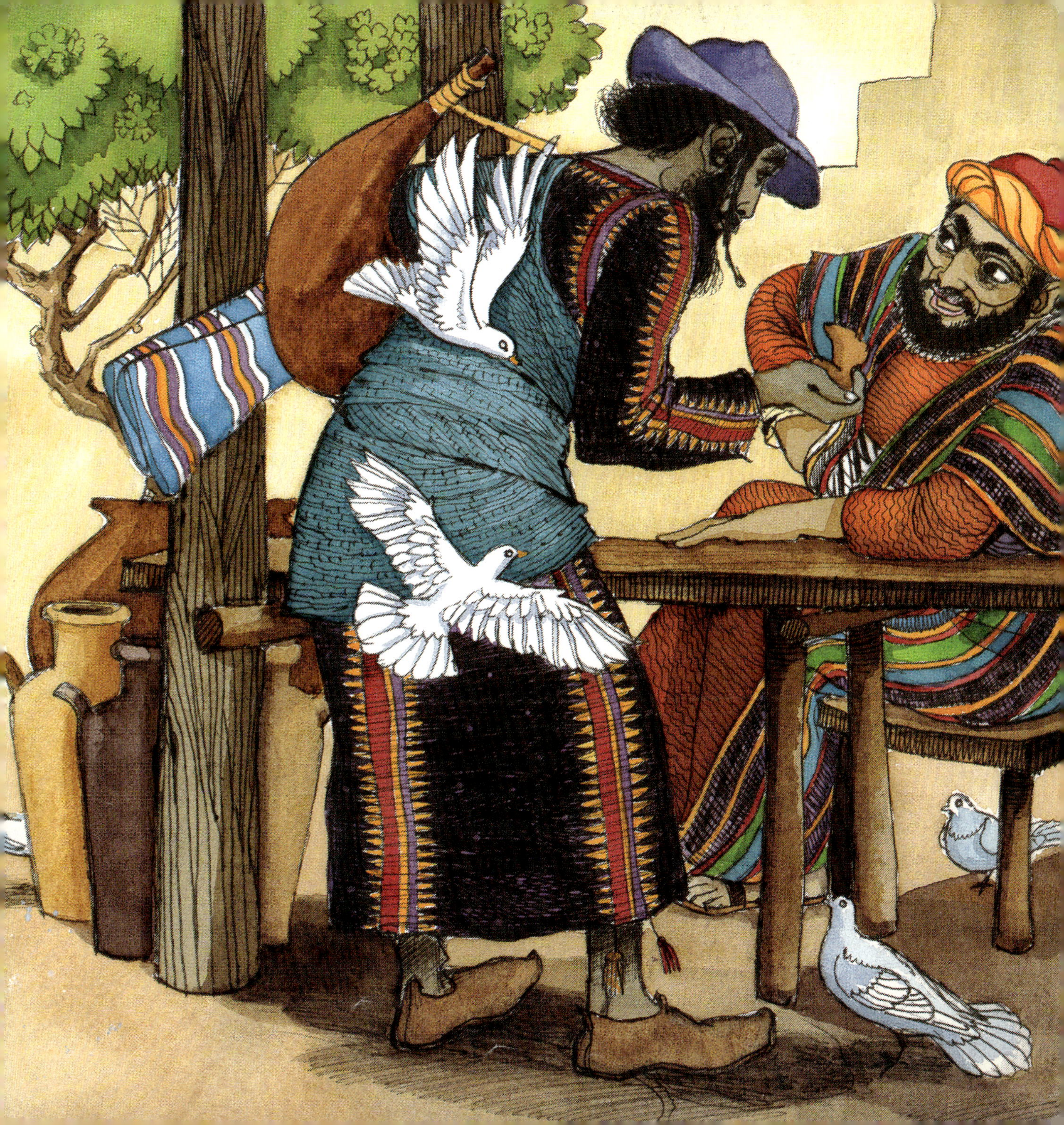

And if you have to spend more than this—
well, I'll repay you on my way back to Jerusalem."

"Oh, don't you worry," said the innkeeper.
"I'll take good care of our friend."

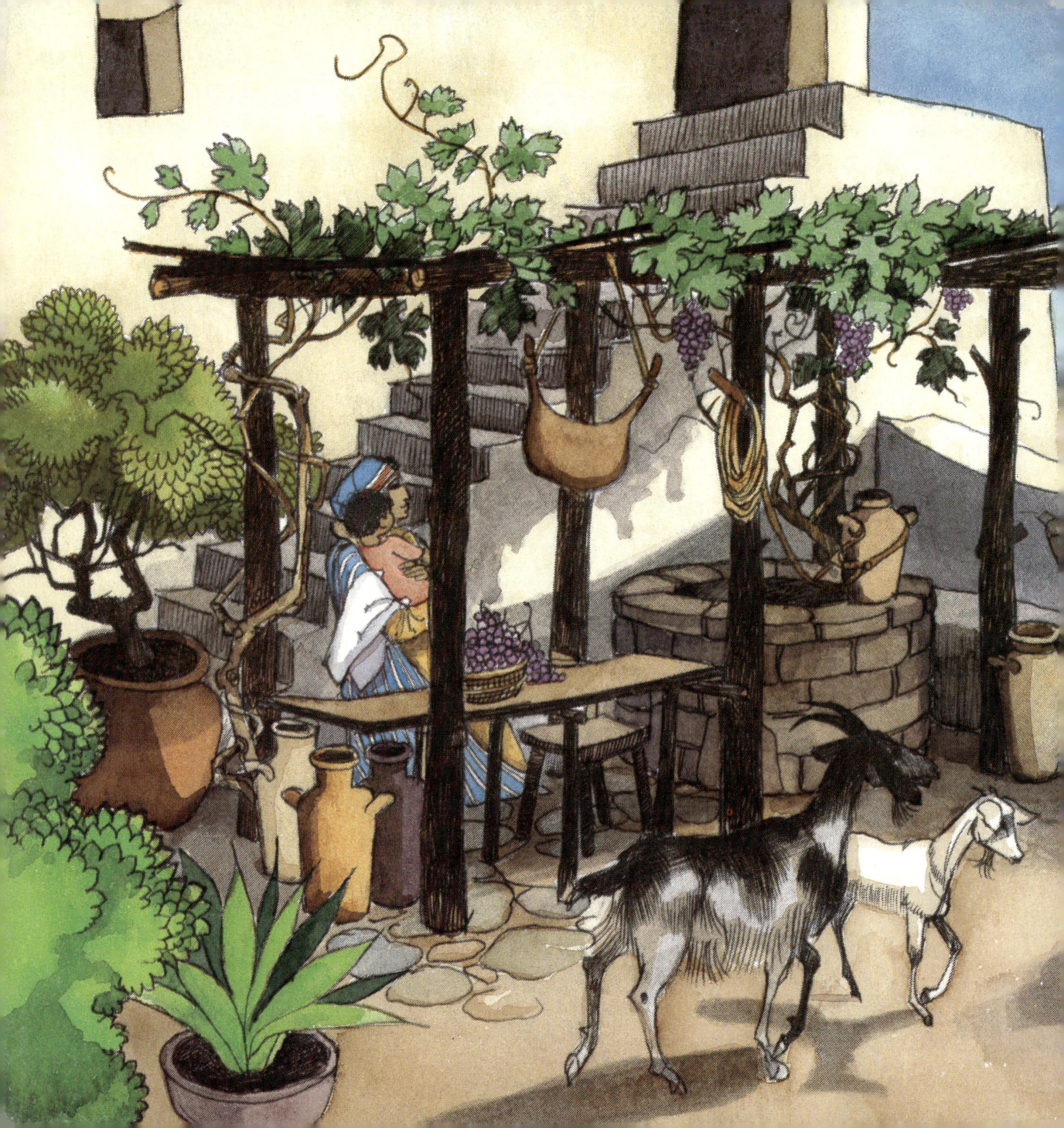

So the Samaritan climbed up happily on his donkey.
And he started off once more
on the steep and lonely, rocky road to Jericho.

That was the end of the parable that Jesus told.

Then Jesus asked the man
   who wanted to know who is a neighbor,
   "Which now of these three do you think
   was the neighbor to the man
   who fell among thieves?"
"Oh, the neighbor was the Samaritan,"
   the man answered.
"He helped the poor fellow, and was kind to him."
"That's right," Jesus said. "Go, and do thou likewise."

WHO IS A GOOD SAMARITAN?
A Song by Merle Witham Miller

Who is a Good Samaritan?
Anyone can be!
If we obey the great commands
God gave you and me.
When we're really loving God
With all our heart and mind,
We are able to help our neighbor —
Sharing good, being kind.

God is the Father of us all,
And our Mother, too.
Jesus the Master showed us why
Love's the Golden Rule.
We'll be Good Samaritans
Every single day, for
God will help us to help each other
In His perfect way.